BARBOZA'S BOOK OF HYPNOTIC INDUCTIONS

John Barboza has fashioned together a handful of easy to do, masterful, creative, hypnotic inductions for your enjoyment.

JOHN BARBOZA

Order this book online at www.trafford.com
or email orders@trafford.com

Most Trafford titles are also available at major online book retailers.

Book design by Diana Grebennikova

Print information available on the last page.

ISBN: 978-1-6987-0401-2 (sc)
ISBN: 978-1-6987-0403-6 (hc)
ISBN: 978-1-6987-0402-9 (e)

Library of Congress Control Number: 2020921364

Trafford rev. 12/08/2020

 www.trafford.com
North America & international
toll-free: 844-688-6899 (USA & Canada)
fax: 812 355 4082

CONTENTS

INTRODUCTION

Hypnosis is quite an interesting and unique phenomenon for those who have never personally witnessed it and for many that have experienced it up close and personal. The same goes for both the newcomers who are just getting their feet wet and the experienced hypnotists. The inductions within these pages will excite the novice as well as the seasoned professional. Each one of the induction techniques has the potential to ignite a spark of curiosity capable of taking you out of your comfort zone and moving you into an entirely new mindset that will give you the confidence to experiment with speed inductions. There are never too many tools you can have in your hypnosis toolbox and I'm certain there will be inductions that will intrigue each inquisitive reader. Whatever induction style you prefer, learning and using any one of the following inductions will improve your skill and add to the knowledge you already possess.

Even if you never use any of the inductions in your office setting or during presentations or when conducting demonstrations, just reading and visualizing the inductions is fun and entertaining. However I'm certain just reading the inductions will not be enough, learning, practicing and utilizing the various techniques within these pages is what's going to excite you. That's what this book is all about. That's why I wrote this book, because of the excitement each induction filled me with when creating them, practicing them, and performing them.

There are over fifty inductions to choose from and many of them can double or triple as instant inductions, rapid inductions or progressive relaxation inductions. For example if you're using a progressive muscle relaxation induction you may find that because the induction is extremely effective and the subject is showing signs of entering hypnosis before you intended her to, you can turn it into a rapid induction or continue on by using the remaining induction process as a deepener.

So in a moment take a deep breath, slowly exhale, close your eyelids for approximately thirty seconds to a minute, and visualize yourself practicing, learning, experimenting and using these inductions. When you have finished, open your eyelids and enjoy reading, learning, and perfecting each induction. Notice the pleasure that comes with the knowledge you are obtaining and apply what you have learned with confidence and excitement as you take yourself, your subjects, and your hypnosis practice to a whole new level.

ACKNOWLEDGEMENTS

Special thanks to everyone involved in this enjoyable time consuming project. Thanks to Jennifer Potts for her spiritual guidance and expeditious reliance whenever called upon in times of my unpredictable immediacy. Thank you Maureen Anderson for being there when most needed and showing tremendous patience in helping me get things right even after fifty bad takes. Your invaluable somnambulistic nature and responses added excitement to each induction. Thank you Jane Woodbridge for taking time out of your busy schedule to help with the editing process. I value your talent and friendship. Thanks to all the staff at Trafford Publishing, you kept me moving forward and gave me that push I needed when I became stagnant. And to all my special hypnotic guinea pigs that helped me fine-tune each induction, if it weren't for all of you, this book would only be a dream, but with your help you made it become a reality. I'm happy to have worked with everyone involved in this project. You all have kept me grounded and I deeply appreciate your contributions and friendships.

And lastly thank you Chris Adshade for contributing your thoughts which were placed within the foreword. I met Chris at an NGH Commonwealth Chapter meeting where he professed his fascination with inductions, especially speed inductions. Soon after, he explained the process and demonstrated an instant induction for the group. Some of the hypnotists expressed their excitement about his hypnosis ability, professionalism, kind nature, humor, and many years of being a hypnotist. After conversing with Chris I thought it would be appropriate to share this project with him in hopes of inviting him to come aboard and express his view of what I have to offer.

INDUCTION

An induction is typically a series of instructions used to produce a trance-like state with the intention of evolving into a hypnotic condition. The induction usually involves suggestions to focus, concentrate, and relax. Inductions are used to shift the consciousness of a person from the external environment inwardly. Any situation where we become absorbed in something moves us towards trance and with the right persuasive elements or conditions, hypnosis can occur. And lastly, inductions can come about or be elicited through shock, boredom, fixation of attention, and relaxation.

TYPES OF INDUCTIONS

There are a few types of inductions that are used to induce a trance or hypnotic state. The first is the instant induction that occurs just as quickly as saying the word sleep. When you unexpectedly tug on the subject's arm, this will startle her, and when you immediately give the command to sleep, this along with the shock causes her to go into hypnosis. Following up with a deepener will increase the intensity of the state she's in.

The next type of induction is the rapid induction. This induction could be the eye lock induction where the person is told to close her eyelids and follow your instructions. Eye catalepsy, which is the inability to open the eyelids, is then suggested. With this type of hypnotic phenomena occurring, simply saying the word sleep after she attempts and fails to open the eyelids, will cause her to drift into hypnosis. Quickly following up with a deepener will keep her moving even further into hypnosis. The different types of rapid inductions could take about a minute to approximately five minutes to induce trance.

The third type of induction is the progressive muscle relaxation induction where the subject is given suggestions to mentally and visually scan and relax each part of her body from her head to her feet. This kind of induction is generally used in the office setting and also during comedy stage hypnosis shows. This type of induction takes several minutes to execute. It is a slow process of relaxing the small and large muscle groups and extremities using visualization techniques and suggestions that lull the subject into a hypnotic trance.

With the progressive muscle relaxation induction, the hypnotist usually starts out by using a permissive approach coaxing the subject into complete physical and mental relaxation. With the instant induction a more aggressive, authoritative approach is used. With the rapid induction, a permissive and or authoritative approach can be used along with challengers such as challenging the person to try and open the eyelids with the intention of having her fail.

DEEPENER

A deepener is a method used to cause the subject to enter a highly suggestible state deep enough that responses to positive suggestions will be achieved. It's essential to seamlessly begin the deepener somewhere near the end of the induction process where trance or hypnosis is imminent.

Deepeners can also be used throughout the hypnotic experience to deepen the hypnotic state to a depth where the subject becomes more open and receptive to suggestions for change. A deepener can be a short suggestion telling the subject to simply go deeper into hypnosis. It can also be as elaborate as a progressive relaxation induction. The subject is directed to mentally scan the entire body focusing on relaxing the muscles in the feet all the way up to the head. A more traditional method is having the subject visualize walking down a staircase of a set amount of steps while being given suggestions to relax. With each movement downward the subject is persuaded to enter a deeper state of relaxation.

HYPNOSIS

Expert practitioners of hypnotism may have varying definitions of what hypnosis is. The following is one of many expressed views.

Hypnosis is a natural human condition which involves a state of heightened awareness, focused attention, and increased response to suggestions.

NOTES

The hypnotee will always be identified as the subject or the female, and the hypnotist will always be identified as the male for the sole purpose of eliminating any confusion between the two of them.

With each induction, after giving the command to sleep or go into hypnosis immediately follow up with a deepener.

Always keep in mind the number one priority which is the safety of the subject. Be aware of any injuries and be sure to prevent injuries from occurring.

Patter is the way you speak or the way you say things in a rapid fire mechanical manner. Some of the inductions include patter which you can memorize and repeat verbatim, while others will require you to create your own interesting chattering talk which preludes or accompanies the induction.

It may be required to repeat or prolong certain sections of some inductions or it may be required to repeat entire inductions more than once in order to induce hypnosis.

SPECIAL DEDICATION

This book is dedicated to Maxi, my best friend
who displayed true friendship and unconditional love,
which in itself is pure hypnosis.

FOREWORD

I am really excited about this book! I am honored to write the foreword to John's book because it teaches you a variety of hypnosis inductions, which happens to be an interest of mine. I have seen a lot of hypnosis books over the many years since I have been a hypnotist. I have truly enjoyed reading this book for the content, style, and format which John presents to the reader.

I met John a couple of years ago when we both attended a hypnotist practice workshop. Many attendees wanted to learn about rapid or instant inductions, so I explained the process and demonstrated a couple of the speed inductions. Later, John approached me and we talked about the inductions I did. While conversing with John I could tell by his questions and his demeanor that he was the type of person who tends to sit back but "takes it all in" and thinks about things and processes them fully. I remember telling John that there are so many hypnotists that are wary to try or use speed inductions and I had felt the same way myself in the past. Many hypnotists see it as being flashy and only beneficial for demos or stage hypnosis. Many are afraid it will not work for them even though they might have been a hypnotist for years.

I tend to use these speedier inductions often because it can be beneficial for both the hypnotist and the client for many reasons. It can benefit the client by being used as a convincer of the hypnosis process, and it can be used as a demo in a therapy session or in a group. Using speed inductions also gives hypnotists more time for the therapy component with their clients. I remember telling John that speed inductions are good and there are so many different inductions that can be used. Sometimes creating an induction or adapting one can stretch the hypnotist's skill level to help their client go into hypnosis.

Unfortunately, many hypnotists learn a variety of inductions but do not use them. Instead, they tend to stick to three or four inductions that they use with every person. They miss the opportunity to broaden themselves by not utilizing the different ways to hypnotize or bring someone into a trance-state. It doesn't have to be speed inductions; it can also be creative styles of inductions. John's book can truly be used to change this for the new hypnotist and the seasoned (veteran) hypnotist. John has a variety of styles of inductions in his book that can teach and benefit the hypnotist and let them grow. What better way to grow than with the hypnosis induction process!

Now to get into some specifics about John's book that makes it a valuable resource for the hypnotist. John briefly explains hypnosis, inductions, and deepeners as well as information that most hypnotists are familiar with. I see many hypnosis books use all this as fluff, explaining these topics in detail. What impressed me about John's book is he did not take up a major portion of the book to do this; instead, he explained those areas briefly and then jumped into the creative induction content.

The book categorizes the types of inductions, and then under each category are the golden nuggets of creative and exciting techniques. Each of these induction "gems" is concisely explained. John presents each induction step-by-step making it easy to learn the process. Even though it is described step-by-step, once familiar, the hypnotist can add variation and personal style to the process. The book's descriptions are "user-friendly" for the newer hypnotist as well as the hypnotist who has been in the field for many years.

After reading this book, you can use it as a great reference tool and jump to a particular section or induction. You can refresh your memory and try a new induction instead of relying on the same few you may have been using. I would suggest keeping this book within arm's reach and challenging yourself to try the different inductions in this book. I am excited to learn and use these inductions myself and I challenge you to do the same.

Learn these inductions.... Use these inductions... and see yourself grow as a hypnotist!

Chris Adshade
Certified Hypnotist

OPPOSITE INDUCTION

Patter:

Articulate to the subject, "In order to get hypnotized it is extremely important to follow simple instructions. In order for you to follow the simple instructions I am about to give you, you have to place your undivided attention on my requests, because you have to do the opposite of everything I tell you to do. So if I tell you to blink - don't blink, or if I tell you not to blink - blink." Test the subject to see if she understands by telling her to blink. If she doesn't blink tell her not to blink. Once she blinks and demonstrates that she understands, proceed with the induction.

Induction:

Tell the subject to open her eyelids. She will close her eyelids. Tell her to close her eyelids. She will open her eyelids. Have her exhale. She will inhale. Tell her to inhale. She will exhale. Now tell her to open her eyelids. When she closes her eyelids, in an authoritative voice immediately command her to sleep by saying, "And don't…Sleep!" as you gently but firmly touch her forehead.

INDEX FINGERS INDUCTION

Set-up:

Standing in front of the subject, have her extend her arms and hands straight out in front of her body with the palms facing forward as though she is gesturing for you to stop moving towards her. Ask her to close her fingers on both hands into fists, except for the index fingers which are to remain protruding outward. Tell her to close the gap between the two hands so the index fingers are side by side touching each other and pointing upward towards the ceiling. Have her bend the arms allowing the hands to move closer to her, stopping approximately six inches away from her face. The fingertips should be at eye level and she should be looking directly at the fingernails of the two index fingers. You are now ready to present the induction.

Induction:

Keeping her head straight forward, direct the subject to simultaneously and slowly move the right hand to the right side and the left hand to the left as far as they are able to go. While keeping her eyes fixated on both fingers, convince her that the slow outward movement of the hands and eyes along with the intense concentration causes her eyelids to tire and close. As she continues using her peripheral vision, encourage eye fatigue, heaviness of the arms and eyelids, and blurred vision. Tell her that when she feels the arms and eyelids getting heavy, her eyelids will close and her arms will move downward. When you see her arms move downward and her eyelids close, command her to sleep.

EYE BLINK INDUCTION

Induction:

Have the subject gaze into your eyes and tell her that every time she blinks she is to whisper, "My eyes are tired - close them and sleep." As she blinks and whispers, help her along by utilizing the pacing and leading technique. First, pace her eye movements or imitate her blinks and then lead the way by acting as if your eyelids are getting heavy and are about to close. The moment she begins imitating your eye movements, you can pretend that your eyelids are tiring, getting heavier and sluggish, and are staying closed longer. When her eyelids look fatigued, slowly close your eyelids and sigh. She may or may not sigh. Seconds after you sigh, slowly peek through your closed eyelids to see if her eyelids are closed. If they are open, tell her to close them and sleep. When they are closed lead her deeper into hypnosis.

THE DOT INDUCTION

Induction:

Take a blank sheet of paper and make a dot in the center of it. Have the subject sit up straight with her head facing forward. Place the sheet on the table approximately twelve inches in front of her. Tell her to lower her eyes and try to stare at the dot without blinking. Let her know that as soon as she blinks the blinking will occur more frequently and she will find that each blink will cause her eyelids to struggle to stay open. She is to give great effort into preventing her eyelids from closing for as long as she can. Tell her that the more she tries to keep the eyelids open the heavier they become, and the moment they close deep hypnosis will follow.

As the subject stares at the dot encourage eye fatigue, strain, blurred vision, and heaviness of the eyelids. As you closely monitor each blink, inform her that her breathing will slow down and the steady fixation of attention will succumb to the closing of the eyelids. Your continuous suggestions will lead the subject into hypnosis.

THE WALK - AROUND INDUCTION

Patter:

The following sentence (Patter 2) should flow as smoothly as you are about to read it. The sentence and your actions should start and end at the same time.

Patter 1: (Should be explained before your trek around the subject begins.)
"I'm going to walk around you and when you can no longer see me close your eyelids. And when I return to this position you will be deeply hypnotized."

Patter 2:
"With your head and body remaining still, follow me with your eyes, and when you can no longer see me close your eyelids and sleep."

Induction:

As you position yourself in front of the subject, instruct her to stand firmly with her arms down by her sides as she stares into your eyes. Her eyes will follow your movements as her head and body remain still. Tell her you are going to walk around her, and as you walk out of her view, she is to close her eyelids. When you return to the position in front of her she will be deeply hypnotized.

As you begin your tour around the subject verbalize your bodily movement and her eye movements as you approach her and walk out of her view. The verbiage, (Patter 2) should be as follows, "With your head and body remaining still, follow me with your eyes, and when you can no longer see me close your eyelids and..."

When you are behind the subject surreptitiously reach your arm and hand out in front of the subject's head. Quickly and gently cover her eyes and forehead with your open hand as you simultaneously support the back of her head with your other hand while finishing the sentence with the word, "...sleep!"

Note:

Again to clarify, as you begin your tour around the subject start out by saying, "With your head and body remaining still, follow me with your eyes..." Standing beside the subject and moving out of her peripheral vision behind her, continue on by saying, "...and when you can no longer see me..." At this moment you should be out of her sight and she should be closing her eyelids. Continue by saying, "...close your eyelids and..." Simultaneously while reaching your arm and hand out in front of the subject's head and covering her eyes, finish the sentence by saying, "...Sleep!"

COMBINATION LOCK INDUCTION

Patter:

"Imagine for a moment your hand is a lock and that lock has a combination which involves a finger movement sequence that opens the door to your subconscious mind. Whenever you use the combination sequence, each finger movement triggers a relaxation response that causes your eyelids to tire and close. This will make you go deeply into hypnosis the moment the combination is completed."

Process:

Demonstrate and explain to the subject that her hand can remain open or closed and she can have the palm or back of her hand facing her. It doesn't matter. What matters the most is using the correct finger sequence combination and the right lock. She can determine the preferred lock by choosing the right or left hand. Have the subject focus her attention on her hand/lock to decide what sequence of finger movements will cause her to become hypnotized. (e.g. slight movement of the thumb, then the middle finger, the pinky, index finger, and finally the ring finger.) Now that she has determined the sequence she is ready to be hypnotized.

Induction:

Have the subject take a slow, deep breath as she stares at her hand while going over the finger sequence in her mind. As she exhales, have her physically begin the finger movement sequence which will cause eye fatigue, heaviness of the eyelids, slow blinking, eye closure, and then hypnosis.

Note:

Some subjects may require additional encouragement and/or a few repetitions of the finger sequence to enhance the results that lead to hypnosis. If this is the case, have the subject continue staring at her hand while she repeats the finger movements as you carry on with the fatigue, heaviness of the eyelids, slow blinking, eye closure, and steady breathing suggestions.

P.O.A. INDUCTION

Pre-induction:

Before you conduct this rapid induction you can set the scene by letting the subject know the induction is going to work extremely fast. It's going to happen so quickly that it's important for the subject to know she will remain standing at all times, even when she closes her eyelids and goes deeply into hypnosis the moment she hears you say the word "sleep."

Induction:

While setting up the safety parameters and priming the subject for hypnosis with the pre-induction patter, you should also be instructing her to separate her feet for maximum balance and stability. Once the preliminaries are given, without attracting too much attention to your retracting movements, you should have distanced yourself approximately four feet away from the subject. This can easily be accomplished by making it appear that you are simply stepping back to monitor her compliancy with your orders. As you begin the induction process have the subject look directly into your eyes. As you take a deep breath tell her to inhale deeply and to exhale when she's ready. When she exhales, immediately and authoritatively move towards her. Enter her personal space by bringing your face inches from hers, then quickly blow a *puff of air* at her and command her to "sleep."

Note:

Milliseconds after blowing the puff of air into the subject's face quickly bring your hands up towards her face. While opening your hands and extending your fingers, command her to "sleep." Immediately after, continue slowly moving your hands downward between the two of you, from your head approximately to the bottom of your chest area. Repeatedly tell her to sleep three to five times as the undulating motions of your hands appear to trace an imaginary set of stacked hourglasses. The rapid upward movements of your hand and fingers will startle the subject, and the downward waving movements will add a dramatic flair to the induction.

P.O.A. Connotes Puff of Air

DOUBLE PALM INDUCTION
(Alternative to the P.O.A. induction)

Pre-induction:

Before you conduct this rapid induction you can set the scene by letting the subject know the induction is going to work extremely fast. It's going to happen so quickly that it's important for the subject to know she will remain standing at all times, even when she closes her eyelids and goes deeply into hypnosis the moment she hears you say the word "sleep."

Induction:

While setting up the safety parameters and priming the subject for hypnosis with the pre-induction patter, you should also be instructing her to separate her feet for maximum balance and stability. Once the preliminaries are given, without attracting too much attention to your retracting movements, you should have distanced yourself approximately four feet away from the subject. This can easily be accomplished by making it appear that you are simply stepping back to monitor her compliancy with your orders. As you begin the induction process have the subject look directly into your eyes. As you take a deep breath tell her to inhale deeply and to exhale when she's ready. When she exhales, immediately and authoritatively move towards her. Once you enter her personal space quickly and surprisingly place both of your palms inches away from her face while commanding her to sleep.

Note:

Milliseconds after commanding her to sleep slowly move your hands downward between the two of you, from your head, approximately to the bottom of your chest area. Repeatedly tell her to sleep three to five times as the undulating motions of your hands appear to trace an imaginary set of stacked hourglasses. The rapid upward movements of your hands towards her face will startle the subject, and the downward waving movements will add a dramatic flair to the induction.

FINGER TAP INDUCTION

Process:

Tap your index finger on the table to clarify how you want the subject to tap her finger. You can begin by telling her you are going to choose the number three and you are going to tap your finger five times. Each time you tap, explain and demonstrate what you expect her to do. Tap and say the number one so she can see and hear it. Tap and say the number two so she can see and hear it. When you tap the chosen number three, leave the finger on the table approximately five seconds longer than when you tap with the other numbers not chosen. Tap and say the number four so she can see and hear it, and finally tap and say the number five so she can see and hear it. The following induction will actually include five chosen numbers. The important point to remember is each time the subject taps and says the numbers she chooses, she is to hold the finger down approximately five seconds longer than she does with the numbers not chosen.

Induction:

Have the subject place her relaxed hand on a surface such as a table, with the heel of her cupped hand and fingertips against the surface. Have the subject pick five numbers out of fifteen in sequence (e.g. 2...4...6...8...10). Explain to the subject that when she begins counting from one to fifteen, she will begin tapping her index finger on the table surface. As she reaches each of the numbers she has chosen, she is to hold the finger down approximately five seconds longer than she does when tapping with the numbers not chosen. Once explained and understood, have the subject fixate her eyes on the index finger and begin tapping and counting. While tapping and counting, encourage deep relaxation, and suggest that the tapping finger is getting very heavy. Insist that each time the chosen numbers are tapped the finger appears to rest longer and the counting of the numbers causes eye fatigue, tiredness, eye closure, deep relaxation, and hypnosis.

Note:

The following is an explanation of how the above example numbers chosen (e.g. 2...4...6...8...10) should be executed. While fixating her attention on her index finger, the subject should tap and say the number one, quickly lifting the finger from the table. When tapping and saying the number two, her finger should rest on the table approximately five seconds longer before lifting it off of the table because that was one of the chosen numbers. The subject should then tap and say the number three, quickly lifting the finger from the table. When tapping and saying the number four, her finger should rest on the table approximately five seconds longer before lifting it off of the table because that was also one of the chosen numbers. She should then tap and say the number five, quickly lifting the finger from the table. When tapping and saying the number six, her finger should rest on the table approximately five seconds longer before lifting it off of the table because that was also one of the numbers chosen. She is to continue this entire process with the intention of reaching the number fifteen. The subject should enter hypnosis well before reaching that number. If she does reach the number fifteen, simply have her start over beginning with the number one.

COPYCAT INDUCTION

Induction:

Tell the subject to do exactly what you do, and stress the point that if she does as asked she will enter a deep profound state of hypnosis. Instruct her to adjust her feet shoulder width apart, and have her place her arms down by her sides making sure her head is facing forward. Position yourself directly in front of her approximately a distance of three feet and place your feet shoulder-width apart. Gaze into the subject's eyes and once again reiterate the importance of mimicking your behavior in order for her to experience deep profound hypnosis.

Spend a moment in complete stillness gazing into her eyes without blinking as she stares back. When you feel the need to blink, inhale loudly and deeply through your nostrils. As she inhales loudly through her nostrils, continue your gaze as she fully completes her inhalation. Exhale loudly through your pursed lips so that she can do the same. Once she has finished exhaling, close one eye and inhale loudly once again through your nose. As she closes one eye and is close to completing her inhalation, release your breath through your pursed lips. Once she is done exhaling, close the other eye so both of your eyelids are closed and inhale deeply and loudly. When she gets close to completing her loud inhalation, exhale loudly and listen for her exhalation. Her exhalation will be your cue to secretly open your eyelids and immediately touch her shoulder, head, or face area while commanding her to sleep.

Note:

When inhaling and exhaling, it's important to breathe loudly throughout the entire process so that she can do the same. The purpose of this is to audibly know when both of her eyelids are closed during the last exhalation. With both of your eyelids closed, you cannot visibly see her eyes, so her third loud exhalation will indicate to you that both of her eyelids are closed. It will also be your cue to open your eyelids so that you can immediately complete the induction before she has a chance to fully exhale.

FINGER HOOK INDUCTION

Process:

When demonstrating how to link the fingers together, have both hands in front of you. The tops of your hands should be facing the ceiling and the palms should be facing the floor. Now make two fists. The thumbs should be touching each other. Turn the hands so that the tips of the thumbs are now touching each other and the knuckles of the index fingers are touching each other and the knuckles of the middle fingers are touching each other and the knuckles of the ring fingers are touching each other along with the knuckles of the pinky fingers touching each other. The pinkies or little fingers should be away from you and the thumbs should be closer to your body. When demonstrating how to hook the fingers move the fists apart and extend the pinkies so the tips of the little fingers are touching each other. For demonstrational purposes, we will slightly move the right pinkie forward away from you so the two pinkies are now positioned to link up with each other. Now hook the little fingers together. The same shall be done with the other fingers during the induction when it is their turn to link up.

Induction:

While showing the subject how she should place her fingers in order to become hypnotized, have her follow along. Hook the two pinkies together, take a slow deep breath, hold it for a few seconds, exhale, and then release them. Now link the ring fingers together, inhale, hold your breath for a few seconds, exhale, and release them. Do the same with the middle fingers, link them together, take a slow deep breath, hold it for a few seconds, exhale, and then release them. Once she understands what to do have her start over and continue on with the induction.

Have her focus her attention on her hands as she hooks the pinkies. Remind her to inhale, hold her breath, exhale, and release the pinkies. As she continues on her own, tell her that the slow methodical linking of the fingers, the slow deep breaths, and the separating of the fingers, along with the deep concentration, will cause her to become weary, sleepy, tired, and drowsy. Tell her that the task is becoming difficult and she is becoming overwhelmed by the relaxing feelings. Mention how her heavy, tired eyelids are straining to remain open, and tell her to notice how she is beginning to drift into hypnosis as she closes her eyelids.

Note:

If the subject's eyes are still open after she finishes going through the entire process of linking all of the fingers, including the thumbs, simply have her repeat the process until the eyelids close.

HAND CATALEPSY INDUCTION

Induction:

Tell the subject to open her hand and spread her fingers apart. Have her stare at the hand and imagine the fingers slowly moving closer together. Persuade her to continue staring at her hand while waiting for the fingers to move of their own accord. Continue to convince her that the fingers will slowly begin to move closer together. Notice any movement or twitch and combine it with the intent. When the fingers meet, tell her to envision them sticking and fusing to each other as they become stiff and rigid and locked together. As the stiffness travels from the fingernails up the fingers to the palm and the wrist, tell her to notice how the entire hand is now stiff, rigid and locked in place. The observance of the subject and the hand actions will help you to determine the direction you take. If you need to spend more time on one particular part of the induction or move ahead, you'll be able to tell depending on the compliancy of the subject. Tell her you are going to have her try and bend the fingers and close them into a fist but she will find it impossible to do so. Tell her to try and as she struggles, ask her if it is difficult. The moment she says yes, command her to sleep.

HYPNAGOGIC JERK INDUCTION

Pre-induction:

Before demonstrating the actions required to go into hypnosis see if the subject has ever experienced a jerk-like sensation of the body while falling asleep. If she has experienced it have her tell you what it was like. After she shares the details of her experience explain how the quick jerk or involuntary contraction of the muscles occurs as a person is falling asleep. Mention how the sudden jerk awakens and then propels the person to sleep. This hypnagogic jerk is also known as a hypnic jerk, sleep start, sleep twitch, myoclonic jerk and a night start. Lastly let her know that this hypnagogic jerk can also be used to thrust a person into hypnosis.

Demonstration:

Demonstrate to the subject how you would like her to slowly inhale through her nose then forcefully blow a short burst of air through her pursed lips as if she were going to whistle or blow out a candle. Tell her that as she does this she will also accompany the puffs of air with a quick jerky motion of certain parts of her body. After a brief demonstration continue on with the induction. A brief example of the induction below can be used as the demonstration.

Induction:

As the subject sits comfortably in front of you with her feet flat on the floor and her hands resting comfortably on her lap, tell her to close her eyelids, slowly inhale through her nose, and then forcefully blow a short burst of air through her pursed lips. While doing this she should also be quickly jerking the left heel of her foot off of the floor and instantly placing it back onto the floor. As she does this she should be imagining a wave of relaxation quickly traveling up her left leg, through her body, to her head, allowing the feeling of relaxation to linger within the body. Have her slowly inhale through her nose and forcefully blow a short burst of air through her pursed lips while quickly jerking the right heel of her foot off of the floor and then instantly placing it back onto the floor. As she does this she should be imagining a wave of relaxation quickly traveling up her right leg, through her body, and to her head, before experiencing another lingering effect of relaxation. She should then slowly inhale through her nose and forcefully blow a short burst of air through her pursed lips while quickly jerking the left heel of her left hand off of her lap, instantly placing it back onto her lap. As she does this she should be imagining a wave of relaxation quickly traveling up her left arm, through her body, to her head. She should then immerse herself in the after effects. Next, she should slowly inhale through her nose and forcefully blow a short burst of air through her pursed lips while quickly jerking the right heel of her right hand off of her lap and then instantly placing it back onto her lap. As she does this she should be imagining a wave of relaxation quickly traveling up her right arm, through her body, and to her head, as the rush of relaxation lingers within her body. And finally, have her slowly inhale through her nose then forcefully blow a short burst of air through her pursed lips while quickly jerking her entire body into hypnosis.

Post-induction:

After the full body hypnagogic jerk occurs, use this time to spread the relaxation throughout her entire body and create, via suggestions, hypnic aftershocks to further deepen hypnosis. Utilize your observance of every twitch and incorporate it into the deepener.

SIMON SAYS INDUCTION

Process:

Simon Says is a children's game where participants are given instructions to follow. The instructions should only be followed if prefaced with the phrase, "Simon says." If you fail to follow these instructions you will be eliminated from the game. If I say, Simon says close your eyelids, you may close your eyelids. If I tell you to close your eyelids without first saying Simon says, and you close your eyelids, you will be eliminated from the game. After explaining the rules, follow up with the induction.

Induction:

Begin the induction by saying, "Simon says close your eyelids." The subject should close her eyelids. The next instruction given is, "Open your eyelids." The subject's eyelids should remain closed. The remaining commands succeed the Simon says phrase. "Simon says inhale." The subject should inhale. "Simon says exhale." She should exhale. "Simon says sleep!"

When saying the word sleep, you should surprise the subject by saying it forcefully while at the same time applying your hands on the subject's shoulder and forehead. Deepen the hypnotic state while slowly rocking her side to side.

THE ALPHABET INDUCTION

Pre-induction:

Go through the alphabet and have the subject imagine hearing, tasting, experiencing, feeling, or visualizing something that starts with the letter given. Once she hears, tastes, smells, feels, or visualizes something, she is to articulate what it is. You can start out with the first few letters of the alphabet and then shift to letters that may elicit a visual, auditory, kinesthetic, olfactory, or gustatory response. The following example in the induction section below explains this more clearly.

Induction:

Have the subject close her eyelids and tell her you are going to say a letter of the alphabet. Tell her she is to visualize something that starts with that letter. When she sees the image she is to tell you what it is. If you say the letter A and the subject imagines seeing an apple, you can follow up by asking her what color the apple is and perhaps the size or even the taste of it. According to her responses you can continue having her elaborate or you may go on to the next letter in sequence or you can choose any letter that you might feel will elicit a sensory response. The letter P for example may be used next to surreptitiously lead, guide, or coax her in the direction of talking about pies, perhaps grandma's secret apple pie recipe. Questions about where she got the recipe from or the aroma of the baked pie might trigger numerous sensory responses that may cause memories to resurface, possibly taking her back to a time in her past. Once the subject exhibits a few of the sensory signs, hypnosis should occur immediately upon your request.

SPIRAL INDUCTION

Induction:

On a blank sheet of paper, starting from the center of the sheet, have the subject carefully begin drawing a spiral. Express the importance of keeping the lines close to each other without letting them touch. Encourage tiredness of the eyes, muscle fatigue of the arm and hand, and heaviness of the eyelids. As the spiral begins to take shape, insist that she is getting very tired and sleepy. When the hand movement ceases, and the eyelids close, tell her to sleep.

HEAVY ARM INDUCTION

Induction:

Have the subject bend and raise her arm so that her hand is approximately twelve inches away from her face about eye level. Now have her fixate her attention on her palm. As she stares at her hand, start out by clearly repeating the following suggestion to her, "Your arm is getting heavy and tired." As you continue to convince her that her arm is getting heavy and tired, inconspicuously remove the word arm and slip in the word eyes the moment you detect fatigue of her eyelids. Eventually as you notice heaviness of the arm and or eyelids, interchangeably go back and forth repeating the heaviness and tiredness of the arm and eyes each time you notice her struggling to control them. As the fatigue continues to grow stronger, monitor the lowering of the arm and the struggle to keep the eyes open. Eventually focus more on convincing her of the heaviness and tiredness and closure of the eyelids. Once the eyelids close, if the arm still has a way to go before settling down by her side or on her lap, use the lowering of the arm as a deepener.

IDEOMOTOR RESPONSE INDUCTION

Induction:

Have the subject stare at her hand while you repeatedly tell her that her fingers, hand, or arm will intermittently begin twitching. The moment a twitch occurs tell her the spasms will continue to increase in frequency and intensity. When this happens have her close her eyelids. Mention that if she tries to stop the tremors she will be unsuccessful. Tell her, the more she tries to make them stop, the more they will continue. Now have her try to stop the spasms so she can see for herself. When she tries to stop the twitching, remind her that the frequency and intensity will increase. As the spasms continue, tell her to take a slow deep breath. As she exhales tell her to notice how the twitching is beginning to slow down. Mention that as the twitching slows down she will begin go into hypnosis, and when the twitching completely stops, she will be deeply hypnotized.

FLOATING HAND INDUCTION

Patter:

"Look right here at the center of my palm as the hand begins to float away. Watch it float, float, float…Sleep!"

Induction:

Standing on the right side of the seated subject, place the palm of your right hand approximately six inches in front of her eyes. With your left hand take your index finger and point to the center of your palm and tell the subject, "Look right here at the center of my palm as the hand begins to float away. Watch it float, float, float…Sleep!"

When you start the patter, the moment you say the first word, "Look" you should be pointing, touching and sticking your left index finger to the center of your right palm. Continue on with the sentence, "…right here at the center of my palm as the hand begins to float away. Watch it…" When you begin to say the word float three consecutive times, simultaneously begin to move your hand up and away from the subject's face as she continues focusing her attention on your palm. As this is happening, at the same time you should be inconspicuously moving your left hand towards the back of the subject's head. All in one fluid motion after reaching the back of the head, move the open hand up towards the top of the head, and then across the top, and finally down past the subjects forehead, and over her eyes. You should be saying the word, "Sleep!" while the palm makes contact with her eyes, guiding them into the closed position.

COMPLIANCY INDUCTION

Induction:

Tell the subject that compliancy is being submissive or eager to please. Then ask her if she knows how to follow the rules of compliancy. The moment she answers yes, place your open hand approximately six inches in front of her eyes slightly above eye level and say to her, "Then focus on the center of my palm." Approximately fifteen seconds later tell her to inhale. When she fully inhales tell her to exhale and close her eyelids. When she closes her eyelids, say to her, "As you inhale lift your hands up towards your face." As she inhales, the moment she begins to move her hands, tap her forehead and tell her to sleep. Her hands should discontinue the movement upwards as she goes into hypnosis.

THE ARM INDUCTION

Induction:

Have the subject extend her arm out in front of her with the palm facing down towards the floor and the fingers spread apart. Tell her to focus her full attention on a point on her hand, and tell her to be certain not to allow her eyes to wander. After a moment passes, ask her what she notices about her arm, hand, or fingers. Does she notice heaviness in her shoulder or tingling in her fingertips? Whatever she notices have her describe it in detail as her eyes remain fixated on her hand. Every once in a while slip in any of the details she shared with you. For instance, if she mentioned that her arm felt heavy and numb, convince her that the heaviness is increasing and causing the arm to move downward. As she reveals other noticeable things occurring, combine those things with what you are influencing her to also experience. At some point convince her that the downward movement of the arm, or the tingling sensation in her hand, or whatever else she may be experiencing, is also causing her eyelids to get heavy with every blink. When the eyelids close suggest she go into hypnosis.

SHAPE SHIFTER INDUCTION

Induction:

Show the subject a pen or any other item and describe the features of it like the size, color, shape, etc. Once you've demonstrated what she will be doing, have her stare at something such as a lamp or paperweight or some other item. As she focuses on the object have her describe it in detail. When she has given a fairly sufficient amount of details have her close her eyelids and imagine that she can still see the object. Tell her to describe it once again in her mind's eye. After describing the item tell her to imagine changing the shape, size, color and anything else about it into another form.

As she describes the changes, gradually begin to direct your questions and or suggestions about the object more towards her. Shift everything away from the object and make it more about her feelings, experiences and relaxation. For instance, if she was focusing on a fan and she shifted it into a boat, have her imagine sailing in the boat in the middle of a pond as she enjoys the morning sunrise. You can then transfer the stillness of the water and the warmth of the light rays from the sun into her body, increasing her awareness of relaxation, inner peace, and calmness. Have her experience these sensations that will eventually transform into relaxation of her body and mind which in turn will lead her into hypnosis.

HAND OR EYES INDUCTION

Patter:

"Notice your eyes are getting tired... Your eyelids are getting heavy... Notice my fingers curving downward...As your eyelids close, my fingers close...tighter and tighter – tightly closed – locked – they cannot open... In a moment I'm going to count from one to three and when I reach the number three you'll try and open your eyelids and you'll find that you cannot open them. One, two and three, try and open those eyelids now. You cannot open them. That's right. Stop trying now and relax those eyelids and allow that relaxation to flow down your entire body, causing you to relax all over."

Induction:

With your arm bent, fingers close together, and fingertips pointing upward towards the ceiling, as though you are waving at the subject, tell her to look at your hand and focus her full attention on the center of your palm. Continue on by saying the following, adding a slight pause in between each directive. "Notice your eyes are getting tired... Your eyelids are getting heavy... Notice my fingers curving downward..." Let the fingers slowly begin to curve downward eventually turning into a fist. "As your eyelids close, my fingers close..." As you carefully watch the eyelids close, let your fingers mimic her eye closure movements until both, her eyelids and your fist are tightly closed.

Now that the eyelids are closed, the pace and continuance of the following directives will be spoken in a more authoritative and slightly rapid and mechanical manner. "Tighter and tighter - tightly closed - locked. They cannot open. In a moment I'm going to count from one to three and when I reach the number three you'll try and open your eyelids and you'll find that you cannot open them. One, two and three, try and open those eyelids now. You cannot open them." Once she successfully demonstrates that she cannot open the eyelids, continue on. "That's right. Stop trying now and relax those eyelids and allow that relaxation to flow down your entire body, causing you to relax all over."

STRESS TEST INDUCTION

Induction:

Have the subject place her hands and arms down by her sides as she stands and stiffens her body, imitating the tense effects of stress. Have her intently focus on an object in front of her. Repeatedly suggest that her body is becoming stiff and solid like a statue. Test the rigidity of smaller parts of her body such as her fingers by asking her to try and move them. As each failed attempt of movement occurs, increase the suggestions of stiffness and the testing of larger limbs such as her arms and legs. When the subject fails to move any part of her body including the head, command her to close her eyelids and sleep.

DEEP SLEEP INDUCTION

Process:

Take a moment to explain to the subject that hypnosis is not sleep, then tell her that you are going to replace the word relax with the word sleep. Inform her that every time you say the word sleep, she is to imagine becoming ten times more relaxed. Once she responds with a yes after asking her if she understands, tell her to naturally breathe as she stares into your eyes.

Induction:

Tell her to let the eyelids close as she exhales and to open the eyelids when inhaling. Continue on by telling her that the more she exhales the more the eyelids want to remain closed. Carry on by letting her know that the more she closes her eyelids the heavier the eyelids become. Finish by saying, the heavier the eyelids become, the harder it is to open them. She will eventually keep the eyelids closed as she goes into hypnosis. Every time the eyelids are closed continuously repeat, "Sleep...sleep...go deeply to sleep."

THE GLASS BOX INDUCTION

Pre-induction:

Explain the concept of a popular 90's game to the subject by stating, "In the 90's there was a popular arcade game called the cash booth, money machine, aka the money booth, or the cash cube. It looked similar to a telephone booth. A participant would enter the booth and try to grab hold of as much paper money as possible in a certain amount of time as the banknotes were blown in every direction."

Induction:

After sharing the details of the money booth game, tell the subject to close her eyelids and imagine she is now stepping into the booth. Tell her the money has been replaced with hundreds of white sheets of paper. The sheets of paper are the size of dollar bills that have large black, bold words printed on them. The words relate to sleep, relaxation, and calmness, etc. (The more words you use relating to restfulness, peacefulness and sleep, will make it easier for her to recall or construct similar words. Here is an example of other words you can use; tranquility, peacefulness, rest, drowsiness, reclining, cozy, contentment, comfortable, quiet, relief, wellbeing, and serenity.)

Tell her that when you press the button and say the word go, the papers will be blown into the air and she will grab several sheets. You will then prompt her to read what's on one slip. When she says the first word out loud, you will expound on the word to elicit a response to guide her into hypnosis. For example if she mentions the word sleep, tell her she is feeling sleepy or remind her what being sleepy feels like. When you prompt her to read the next word, if she says the word tired, tell her that her eyes are getting tired and her arms are getting tired. Explain to her what being tired feels like such as feeling lethargic, etc. You can continue having her read a few more words or you can coax her into hypnosis when it feels appropriate to do so.

REFRACTORY SUBJECT INDUCTION

Patter:

"Compliance is a key element needed for hypnosis to work, but in this case I encourage you to defy my suggestions to go into hypnosis. In fact I want you to ignore my three requests to go into hypnosis, because after the third attempt, I will give up and you will win. It's exactly like the moments when you try to force yourself to go to sleep at night. What happens when you try too hard to go to sleep? You can't go to sleep right? But the moment you stop trying to go to sleep you're eyelids close and you immediately go to sleep, right? So let's try. Are you ready?"

Induction:

Now that you've skillfully persuaded the subject to believe she can resist your attempts at hypnotizing her, quietly prove her wrong. Challenge her by snapping your fingers in front of her face while forcefully saying "sleep." Immediately continue on by tapping her forehead and commanding her to sleep. Finally, open your hand so your palm is facing upward towards the ceiling and have her place her palm on top of yours. Tell her to forcefully press down on your hand. The moment she presses down, resist for a second then quickly whisk your hand away while commanding her to sleep.

Once you've completed the three failed attempts, congratulate her for successfully resisting by sheepishly saying, "You win... Good job." As you shake her hand while congratulating her, surprisingly place your left hand over her entire face and say, "Now sleep!"

THE METRONOME INDUCTION

Induction:

Tell the subject to sit comfortably then have her slowly inhale and exhale three times on her own. On the third inhalation tell her to close her eyelids as she exhales. Once her eyelids are closed have her focus her attention on the sound of the metronome which you should activate on cue while saying the word "metronome." As she focuses her attention on the ticking mention that entrainment will occur. Her breathing and heartbeat will at some point naturally become synchronized with the sound. Point out to her that as she continues to intently focus on the metronome, she will begin to differentiate the tick from the tock. Realizing the slight difference, she will soon hear the tick in one ear and the tock in the other ear. Tell her, when she notices the differences, her index fingers on her right and left hands will begin moving up and down to the rhythm of the metronome...right, left, right, left. Once the ideomotor movement occurs, let her know that each sound of the metronome is causing her body to relax. The tick is causing one half of her body to relax while the tock is causing the other half of her body to relax. She will know that her body and mind will be completely at rest soon after the finger movement's stop. It's quite alright to coax her into relaxing the finger movements which will increase full body repose. When the fingers remain still and she is completely at rest, tell her that the moment the metronome sound ceases, the silence will send her into a deep hypnotic trance. Let her know this will cause her body to instantly become ten times more loose, limp, and relaxed.

THE OBJECT INDUCTION

Induction:

Have the subject open her hand so the palm is facing upward toward the ceiling. Tell her you are going to place something in her hand out of her view and she is to firmly wrap her fingers around the object securing it in the center of her closed fist. Once the object is safely secured, fiddle with your cellular phone as though you are searching for something that is related to both the induction and the object located in the subject's hand. After finding what you were pretending to look for, have the subject tighten her grip and stare at her hand as you briefly talk about how smart phones can be used for just about anything nowadays. "Smart phones can make movies, be used as security systems, contact people from around the world, fly drones, and even explode bombs." After convincingly praising the power of the cell phone, tell her you are going to use an app to increase the temperature of the item you placed in her hand, to the point where it will become excruciatingly unbearable to hold. Tell her that the moment it gets too hot, she is to toss it on the floor so it doesn't burn her hand.

Begin moving your finger around the cell phone screen while informing the subject that you are slowly increasing the temperature. Tell her you are going to raise the temperature to a point where she will begin feeling the effects of the mechanism heating up the object in her hand. At this point you can have her close her eyelids or focus on her hand. Continue increasing the temperature, updating her, and convincing her that it is getting hotter and that she should begin feeling a sudden difference in temperature as the numbers continue to rise. Keep raising the numbers, increasing the heat, and giving suggestions of how difficult it is to hold onto the object. Periodically question her about the heat, asking her what it feels like while persuading her to think about releasing the object rather than holding on to it. If her eyes are still open and she begins to show signs of discomfort, or if she looks like she is about to release the object, tell her to close her eyelids and go into hypnosis. If the eyelids are already closed, simply tell her to go into hypnosis.

Note:

Frequency generator smart phone apps that create audible sounds which increase in pitch can be used to suggest the amplification of heat intensity.

TWO HAND STICK INDUCTION

Induction:

Have the subject place both of her palms flat on the table. Have her focus her attention on the area of the table between the two hands and tell her to imagine that the fingers and hands are sticking to the table. Continue with the suggestions of the fingers and palms sticking and bonding to the table. Keep switching back and forth to both hands paying particular attention to the fingers that are stuck. Keep insisting on getting the unstuck fingers to stick to the table. Eventually after spending a fair amount of time convincing the subject that the palms and most or all of the fingers are securely stuck and glued to the table, command her to close her eyelids and sleep.

THE HYPNOTIC BUTTON INDUCTION

Induction:

Tell the subject to extend her arm out in front of her. Once she extends her arm as far as she can reach, have her pretend to touch and press a red hypnotic button. After she imagines pressing the button, have her place her hand and arm on her lap. Now tell her to fixate her eyes on the imaginary hypnotic button. Shortly after, have her close her eyelids as she pretends to gaze at the button behind her tightly closed eyelids. Encourage her to focus on the button and on your instructions to relax with every inhalation and exhalation. As she continues to focus, breathe, and relax, have her imagine that her hand is becoming lighter and the lightness is traveling up her arm. Have her notice any slight twitches that may occur with her fingers, hand, or arm. Inform her that any twitching or movement is a signal coming directly from her subconscious mind directing her hand and arm to lift from her lap and to move towards the red button. Continue to suggest lightness, twitching, lifting, and movement of the hand and arm. As the hand moves closer towards the hypnotic button, make her aware of the increasing, powerful, feeling of anticipation, and the overwhelming sensation of relaxation that is spreading throughout her body. When her arm is fully extended have her press the red hypnotic button. Convince her that she is drifting into a deep wonderful hypnotic sleep as her arm and body begins to become loose and limp and relaxed.

POINTING INDEX FINGERS INDUCTION

Induction:

Instruct the subject to extend her arms and opened hands out in front of her, palms facing downward. Have her close her hands into fists. Tell her to extend and point her index fingers forward. Now have her point the extended fingers towards each other so the tips of the fingers are touching. Have her focus her eyes on the spot where the fingers meet for approximately fifteen seconds. At the end of the fifteen seconds have her inhale deeply. As she exhales tell her to begin slowly moving the fingers apart all the way to the left and all the way to the right creating a huge distance between the two fingers. Remind her to try her best to keep her eyes focused on the fingers as they separate from each other, the left eye following the left finger and the right eye following the right finger. When the arms are fully stretched out tell her to close her eyelids and slowly have the fingers begin their trek back to the original position in front of her where they first joined. Tell her to also visualize the fingers moving as she tries her best to connect the fingertips. As she concentrates on the task of moving the fingers closer together, before they touch, gently force the hands and arms downward and command her to sleep.

SLEEP INDUCTION

Induction:

Have the subject stare at an object in front of her. Let her know that every time she hears you say the word sleep she is to close her eyelids for a few seconds and imagine hearing your voice echoing the word sleep. Her eyes are to remain fixated in the area of the object even while the eyelids are closed. After a few seconds she is to open her eyelids. Inform her that at some point she may find it more difficult to open them. Let her know that eventually she will notice that her eyelids will remain closed and at that point she will go into hypnosis.

After explaining what will occur, begin the induction by telling her to hold her breath after deeply inhaling. When a sufficient amount of time passes, tell her to exhale and sleep. As she exhales she should close her eyelids and imagine hearing the echoing sound of your voice repeating the word sleep. After a few seconds she should reopen her eyelids. The moment she opens her eyelids, tell her to inhale deeply and hold her breath. After a sufficient amount of time passes, tell her to exhale and sleep again.

The next time she opens her eyelids, as she focuses her attention on the object in front of her, have her notice how heavy her eyelids are becoming. Continue on by saying, "When you close your eyelids to sleep..." (Because you mentioned the word "sleep" she should have closed her eyelids. If her eyes are still open repeat the

word sleep so she can close them, and then finish the sentence.) "...
relax and sleep. Allow each exhalation to cause all the muscles in
your body, especially all those tiny little muscles in your eyelids, to
just relax, relax, relax, and sleep." Continue this type of verbiage
when the eyelids open and close until the eyelids remain closed.

THE MENTAL INDUCTION

Induction:

Explain to the subject how important following simple instructions is when involving hypnosis. Enlighten her with a quick demonstration of what she needs to do in order to get hypnotized. Tell her to raise her left hand in the air, and then tell her to lower it to her side. Have her place her right hand in front of her face so she can look at the palm. As she focuses intently on her palm praise her for doing exactly what is needed to go into hypnosis. Now let her know that you are going to give her more instructions, but this time she will mentally follow the instructions the moment she is told to close her eyelids. Have her take a deep breath, and as she exhales tell her to lower her hand to her side and close her eyelids. Now remind her to mentally follow all of your instructions.

Tell her to imagine walking forward. After a brief moment of encouraging her to pretend taking a few steps forward, ask her if she took the steps forward and if she did, ask her which foot she started with. Now tell her to see herself beginning to run up a steep hill. Ask her if she's running, and once she answers yes, ask her at what speed, fast or slow? After a brief moment of encouraging her to imagine running, have her stop and pretend she is about to walk down a spiral staircase. Tell her there are one hundred steps and when she begins walking down the steps she is to verbally count out each step she takes starting with step one hundred down to step one. Once she acknowledges that she understands these instructions have her begin walking down the steps. As she begins walking and counting, at some point maybe around step ninety-seven, tell her to continue counting as you explain the next instruction to her.

Tell her to make believe she is smiling and explain to her that when she thinks about smiling, the muscles in her face begin to react which creates a smile. Without actually telling her to physically smile, covertly coax her into making those muscles in her face smile by encouraging her to imagine what a smile feels like. Give her suggestions to look in the mirror and imagine smiling and even showing off those pearly whites. Continue persuading her to mentally smile until you actually see her physically smile. As she continues walking down the spiral staircase suggest she go deeper into hypnosis. Carry on by telling her to imagine that all the muscles in her body including her facial muscles are relaxing with each step she takes. Tell her that each number and each step causes deep relaxation. Continue by saying, "Relax, relax, relax as you continue going down, down, down, deeper and deeper down, as all the muscles in your body and face relax, relax, relax." The moment the smile is removed from her face suggest she go into hypnosis by saying, "Go deeply into hypnosis now!" Once you command her to go into hypnosis you can carry on with the deepening suggestions by having her continue walking down the stairs.

HANDS AND FEET INDUCTION

Induction:

Have the subject sit with her feet flat on the floor while resting the palms of her hands on her knees. Tell her to press both of her feet down on the floor for maximum contact. Then have her press both of her hands against her knees to also attain maximum contact. Now have her close her eyelids and imagine that one of her extremities is becoming stuck to the surface. Check to see which part of her body is stuck by asking her. Is her left or right foot stuck to the floor or is her right or left hand stuck to a knee? Have her continue imagining the feet sticking to the floor and the hands sticking to the knees. Suggest that the more she tries to lift a foot or hand, the more stuck they become and the more difficult it is for her to lift either one or more extremities. Go back and forth continually convincing her of how difficult it is to lift the hands and feet. Continue rechecking to see which part of her body is stuck. Is her left or right foot stuck to the floor, or is her right or left hand stuck to a knee? The moment she tells you that one of her hands or one of her feet is stuck, command her to go into hypnosis.

POINT AND STARE INDUCTION

Induction:

While standing near the subject, tell her all that's required of her is to look at the things you point to. It's important for your hand to be placed somewhere in the proximity of her vision so when you point at different items she will notice and refocus her attention on each item you point to. Begin by pointing at something such as a book. As she focuses her attention on the book, with your hand still in her sight, begin pointing your finger at something else such as a clock on a wall. As she focuses her attention on the clock, with your hand still in her sight, begin slowly pointing your finger at your shoe. While pointing at your shoe and as the subject is shifting her head and eyes downward, inconspicuously move your other hand completely out of her vision above her head. As she focuses her attention downward at your shoe, with your hand still in her sight, slowly begin pointing your finger at your other hand above her head. As she adjusts her head and eyes upward in the direction of your other hand, quickly and safely bring the hand down over her eyes while giving the command to sleep.

THE THREE STEP INDUCTION

Induction:

Have the subject stand in front of you and explain the instructions to her. Stand fairly close to her and tell her you are going to step back. As you are telling her this, take one step backwards. After stepping back she is to inhale, exhale, close her eyelids, say the number one, and then open her eyelids. After she opens her eyelids tell her you are going to step back a second time. You should be stepping backwards while explaining this to her. After you have stepped backwards, continue telling her she is to inhale, exhale, close her eyelids, say the number two, and then open her eyelids. After she opens her eyelids, you will step back for a third time while telling her you will step back again. After you step back she is to inhale, exhale, close her eyelids, say the number three, and open her eyelids. Tell her that when she opens her eyelids you will say the word sleep and she will close her eyelids and go deeply into hypnosis.

The most important part of this induction is making it clear that the moment she opens her eyelids and you say the word sleep, she is to close her eyelids and go deeply into hypnosis. Now that you have explained the steps required for this induction to work, stand closely in front of the subject. Tell her she will maintain her balance throughout the entire induction keeping her feet firmly planted on the floor. Before actually starting the induction, quickly reiterate the first step by telling her that each time you step back she is to inhale, exhale, close her eyelids, say the number of steps taken, and then open her eyelids. After reminding her of this, begin the induction by stepping backwards. After stepping backwards she will inhale, exhale, and close her eyelids. The moment she closes her eyelids, you are to quietly step forward approximately around the time she is saying the number one. After she says the number one, she will open her eyelids not expecting you to be standing in close proximity of her. The instant she opens her eyelids you are to authoritatively tell her to sleep while quickly placing your hands on her face and head.

MIRROR INDUCTION

Induction:

Have the subject stare at her reflection in a mirror. Tell her, as she stares into the eyes of the reflection, the reflection's stare will cause her eyes to tire. As she watches the eyelids struggling to remain open, tell her each blink will create overwhelming fatigue of the eyelids eventually diminishing all attempts to keep them open. When the last attempt to keep the eyelids from permanently closing is imminent, remind her of how tired and sleepy the eyes are. Finish by telling her, when she closes the heavy, exhausted eyelids, a wonderful, peaceful, relaxing, deep hypnotic sleep will ensue.

TINGLING ARM INDUCTION

Induction:

Have the subject stretch her arm straight up towards the ceiling as though she is reaching for something. Tell her to look up at her opened hand and focus her attention on one of the fingertips. As she is focusing, suggest that she is able to feel the blood rushing from the tips of her fingers down through her hand and arm. Continue increasing her awareness of the blood flowing down from her hand to her wrist through her arm to her shoulder. As you make her aware of the blood flow and tingling sensation of the fingers and hand, also include tiredness of the eyes and heaviness of the eyelids and arm. As you combine the heaviness and tiring of the eyelids and arm, suggest that the eyelids are closing and the arm is gradually descending. As the arm continues its descent towards the floor and the eyelids close, suggest that the lowering of the arm is causing her to relax and go into hypnosis.

THE CHAOTIC INDUCTION

Induction:

This is a great induction to use if you are in a loud environment such as a club. Start out by stating how noisy it is and express the thrill of how great it's going to be to show the subject how sound plays a significant role in inducing hypnosis. Take a few seconds to have her look around to see where the sounds are coming from, and then have her stare into your eyes and take a deep breath. Tell her to exhale while closing her eyelids for the purpose of eliminating any visual stimuli. This will help her to focus more on your voice as the sounds slowly transform into a type of white noise. Have her focus her attention on a certain sound perhaps a laugh or a particular voice. Let her tell you what sound she is singling out. Once she has done that, have her focus on another sound and have her share the details. Make her aware that when she focuses on one specific sound, the other sounds will begin to dissipate.

Now have her focus her full attention on your voice so she can allow all the other sounds to become less noticeable. Tell her the noise will exist but it will not disturb this key moment of complete concentration. In fact have her hear all other sounds as comforting, calming, white noise that causes relaxation to float to the surface as she sinks into a profound state of lethargy. Methodically direct her attention away from the outside noises. Have her focus on the beating of her heart, the moments she inhales and exhales, and how your soft soothing voice produces a deeper state of inner peace. As you lower your voice to a whisper, perhaps getting closer to her ear, begin the progressive relaxation process of systematically relaxing all parts of her body from the head to the feet.

HAND GRASP INDUCTION

Process:

While facing each other adjust your seat so the subject is sitting slightly to your right. The right side of your right knee should be positioned in close proximity to the right side of her right knee.

Induction:

Instruct the subject to sit comfortably with her palms resting on her lap. Rest your left palm on your left leg and place your right hand in front of your body approximately four inches above your right leg with your palm facing up towards the ceiling. Be certain to keep your elbow against your ribcage. Tell the subject to be sure to keep her right elbow against her ribcage. Her right hand (palm facing downward) should be approximately six inches above her leg, a little higher than the height of your right hand floating above your leg. Demonstrate and explain what is going to occur. As she focuses intently into your eyes have her inhale. As she exhales tell her to extend her arm and hand towards your waiting palm. When she reaches your palm, tell her to place her palm down onto your palm. Have her curl her fingers as you curl your fingers so you are both gripping each other's fingers. Release the fingers and tell her to inhale as she returns her arm and hand back to the starting position.

Now tell her to close one eyelid and exhale as she extends her arm and hand towards your open hand. When she reaches your palm, she is to grasp your fingers once again. When you both release the fingers she is to inhale as her arm and hand return back towards her body. She is then told to close both eyelids. Once both eyelids are closed have her exhale as she extends her arm and hand towards your waiting palm. When she reaches your hand, she is to put her palm in your hand and grasp your fingers for the last time. When the grip is released she is to inhale, return her arm and hand to the starting position, and go into hypnosis.

Now that the subject has been made aware of the procedure, tell her that it is time to begin. Tell her to stare into your eyes and inhale. When she is ready to exhale she is to extend her arm and hand towards your waiting palm, and when both palms make contact grasp each other's fingers. When the fingers release tell her to inhale as she returns her arm and hand back to the starting position. She is then told to close one eyelid. As she exhales she should be extending her arm and hand towards your open hand. When she reaches your palm grasp each other's fingers once again. When the fingers release she is to inhale as she returns her arm and hand back towards her body. Now remind her to close both eyelids. Once the eyelids are closed she is to exhale as she extends her arm and hand towards your waiting palm which is nowhere to be found.

It is at this critical moment while observing the subject's facial expressions and monitoring the movement of her arm and hand reaching out in search of your hand, that you slowly and deceptively remove your hand from its position. Turn your palm downward and lift it a few inches higher than hers, keeping it close by so you can quickly take hold of her wrist when the time is right. While simultaneously removing your right hand from its position, extend your left arm and hand towards the right side of the subjects, head. Once she begins to search for your right hand, within a few seconds she should notice something isn't quite right. A look of confusion may appear on her face. Her eyes may squint causing a visible grimace on her face as her hand movement searches for your hand. The moment you detect any of these signs, instantly grab or slightly push her arm downward with your right hand. At the same time you should be touching the back of her neck, shoulder or head areas with your left hand while commanding her to sleep.

Explanation:

Sitting closely and slightly to the right of the subject, evaluate compliancy as you verbally give her basic instructions of how she is to be seated. Once full compliancy is confirmed and you are both seated and positioned correctly, ease any tension by thoroughly explaining the induction process that is about to take place.

Her gaze should be affixed and unwavering, and all of her inhalations should occur while she recoils her arm and hand back towards her body. Eye closure should take place when her arm is resting against her ribcage. It is while extending her arm and hand away from herself towards you, the hypnotist, that all exhalations take place.

HAND GRASP INDUCTION (ALTERNATE ENDING)

Process:

While facing each other adjust your seat so the subject is sitting slightly to your right. The right side of your right knee should be positioned in close proximity to the right side of her right knee.

Induction:

Instruct the subject to sit comfortably with her palms resting on her lap. Rest your left palm on your left leg and place your right hand in front of your body with your palm facing up towards the ceiling approximately four inches above your right leg. Be certain to keep your elbow against your ribcage. Tell the subject to be sure to keep her right elbow against her ribcage. Her right hand (palm facing downward) should be approximately six inches above her leg, a little higher than the height of your right hand floating above your leg. Demonstrate and explain what is going to occur. As she focuses intently into your eyes have her inhale. As she exhales tell her to extend her arm and hand towards your waiting palm. When she reaches your palm, tell her to place her palm down onto your palm. Have her curl her fingers as you curl your fingers so you are both gripping each other's fingers. Release the fingers and tell her to inhale as she returns her arm and hand back to the starting position.

Now tell her to close one eyelid and exhale as she extends her arm and hand towards your open hand. When she reaches your palm, she is to grasp your fingers once again. When you both release the fingers she is to inhale as her arm and hand return back towards her body. She is then told to close both eyelids. Once both eyelids are closed have her exhale as she extends her arm and hand towards your waiting palm. When she reaches your hand, she is to put her palm in your hand and grasp your fingers for the last time. When the grip is released she is to inhale, return her arm and hand to the starting position, and go into hypnosis.

Now that the subject has been made aware of the procedure, tell her that it is time to begin. Tell her to stare into your eyes and inhale. When she is ready to exhale she is to extend her arm and hand towards your waiting palm, and when both palms make contact grasp each other's fingers. When the fingers release tell her to inhale as she returns her arm and hand back to the starting position. She is then told to close one eyelid. As she exhales she should be extending her arm and hand towards your open hand. When she reaches your palm, grasp each other's fingers once again. When the fingers release she is to inhale as she returns her arm and hand back towards her body. Now remind her to close both eyelids. Once the eyelids are closed she is to exhale as she extends her arm and hand towards your waiting palm. When both palms make contact, grasp each other's fingers. When she is ready to inhale and return her arm and hand back to the starting position, do not release her hand. The split second she recognizes something is not right and shows any signs of confusion, instantly control her arm by safely tugging or pushing it downward with your right hand while touching the back of her neck, shoulder or head areas with your left hand as you command her to sleep.

Explanation:

Sitting closely and slightly to the right of the subject, evaluate compliancy as you verbally give her basic instructions of how she is to be seated. Once full compliancy is confirmed and you are both seated and positioned correctly, ease any tension by thoroughly explaining the induction process that is about to take place.

Her gaze should be affixed and unwavering, and all of her inhalations should occur while she recoils her arm and hand back towards her body. Eye closure should take place when her arm is resting against her ribcage. It is while extending her arm and hand away from herself towards you, the hypnotist, that all exhalations take place.

INTERRUPT INDUCTION

Induction:

While standing approximately five feet away from the chair, have the subject sit down. While the subject is sitting and preparing herself to be hypnotized, walk towards her and ask her if she would please stand up for a moment. When she begins to get up from the chair, immediately press down on her shoulders. Gently push her back into the chair while commanding her to sleep.

FALSE HANDSHAKE INDUCTION

Induction:

Approach the subject while she is sitting. When she makes eye contact, glance down at her right hand and extend your right hand outward to initiate a handshake. The moment she extends her hand to shake yours, bypass her hand and move both of your hands up towards her head. Command her to sleep as you lightly grasp her head, cover her ears, and gently rock her head from side to side.

LEFT HAND RIGHT HAND INDUCTION

Induction:

Have the subject place both of her hands either on a table, on her lap, or out in front of her with the palms facing forward and the fingers spread apart pointing up towards the ceiling. As she looks at the back of her hands, tell her you are going to have her count when looking at the fingers on her left hand and you are going to have her say the alphabet when looking at the fingers on her right hand.

Keeping her head straight forward, she is to look at the little finger on her left hand and say the number one. She should now look at her thumb on her right hand and say the letter A. She will then look at her ring finger on her left hand and say the number two, and then she should look at the index finger on her right hand and say the letter B. Once she reaches the fifth finger on each hand, (the thumb on the left hand and the little finger on the right hand), she will return back to the little finger on the left hand. She will then continue with the number six. From there she will look at her thumb on the right hand and say the letter F.

As she continues counting and saying the alphabet while looking at each finger being counted and alphabetized, begin reporting what she is doing and suggest that she will eventually find it difficult to keep track. Watch for signs of eye fatigue, confusion, difficulty focusing, and deep thinking, as she tries to remember the sequence of the numbers and letters. Tell her that at some point the eyelids will close and the numbers and letters will fade as she becomes hypnotized.

LEFT HAND RIGHT HAND INDUCTION (ALTERNATE ENDING)

Induction:

Have the subject place both of her hands either on a table, on her lap, or out in front of her with the palms facing forward and the fingers spread apart pointing up towards the ceiling. As she looks at the back of her hands, tell her you are going to have her count when looking at the fingers on her left hand and you are going to have her say the alphabet when looking at the fingers on her right hand.

Keeping her head straight forward, she is to look at the little finger on her left hand and say the number one. She should now look at her thumb on her right hand and say the letter A. She will then look at her ring finger on her left hand and say the number two, and then she should look at the index finger on her right hand and say the letter B. Once she reaches the fifth finger on each hand, (the thumb on the left hand and the little finger on the right hand), she will return back to the little finger on the left hand. She will then continue with the number six. From there she will look at her thumb on the right hand and say the letter F.

As she continues counting and saying the alphabet while looking at each finger being counted and alphabetized, begin reporting what she is doing and suggest that she will eventually find it difficult to keep track. Watch for signs of eye fatigue, confusion,

97

difficulty focusing, and deep thinking, as she tries to remember the sequence of the numbers and letters. The moment you detect any of these signs, interrupt her concentration by covering her eyes and commanding her to sleep.

THE INSTANT DEEPENER INDUCTION

Induction:

As the subject stands up straight with her arms down by her sides and her feet together, have her take a deep breath and stiffen her legs, arms, neck and the rest of her body. Tell her to close her eyelids, exhale, and remain stiff and rigid as she goes deeply to sleep.

This induction requires an assistant to make sure the subject does not fall to the floor. The spotter should discreetly make his way behind the subject as she closes her eyelids. When you tell her to go deeply to sleep, you should be gently placing your hands on her shoulders. Gently, yet quickly and forcefully push her backwards as you say the word sleep. This is where the assistant spots the subject making sure she only falls back a few inches. He should then slowly guide and sway her backward and downward and then upward, returning her back to the standing position.

Immediately after saying sleep and pushing the subject back, you should be saying, "Stiff and rigid, deeper and deeper down... so deep...so stiff, so rigid, so deeply relaxed." As the spotter begins to guide her back to the standing position, you should begin saying, "Up... up... all the way up, as if you are floating and going deeper and deeper into hypnosis." She should now be standing in the vertical position. Begin lifting her arms up in front of her, guiding the left arm slightly to her left side, and the right arm slightly to the right side of her body about shoulder level. While lifting the arms continue persuading her to go deeper into hypnosis while repeating, "Up... up... all the way up, as if you are floating and going deeper and deeper into hypnosis." Allow the arms to remain in the floating position as she goes deeper into hypnosis.

REVERSE EYE CATALEPSY INDUCTION

Induction:

Direct the subject to roll her eyeballs upward as though she is trying to fixate her attention on her eyebrows. With minimal to no blinking have her concentrate on remaining perfectly still while focusing upward. Tell her to mentally repeat to herself, "I can close my eyelids." As she continues to mentally repeat this sentence while intensely focusing on her eyebrows, tell her you are going to have her try and close her eyelids. Let her know that when she attempts to close her eyelids she will realize they will not close. Tell her that the harder she tries to close her eyelids, the harder it will be for her to close them. Remind her to visually focus on her eyebrows while mentally repeating, "I can close my eyelids." After repeating these instructions to her tell her that she will know when the moment is right for her to *try* and close the eyelids. Let her know that the moment for her to *try* and close her eyelids will be when she is certain the eyelids will not close.

Now tell her to imagine that the eyelids are frozen open and the eyelids feel as though they are glued and stuck to her face. Tell her to imagine that there are no eyelids to close and that the muscles that work the eyelids are stiff and rigid and stuck in the open position. Remind her to focus on her eyebrows and to imagine that the eyelids are stuck open as she continues repeating the sentence, "I can close my eyelids." Tell her to try and close them when she is sure they will not close. The moment she attempts to close the eyelids and finds it impossible to do so, give her the command to stop trying and to close the eyelids, and sleep.

THE ILLUSION INDUCTION

Process:

This induction uses a sleight of hand trick known as, the French Drop. As you appear to take or transfer an object such as a coin from one hand to the other hand, the coin actually never leaves the hand it started in. It is used in close-up magic and will take some practice to perfect. There are many "how to" websites you can learn the French Drop from. Once you learn, practice, and perfect this sleight of hand technique, you will be able to incorporate it into this induction and use it with people of all ages.

Induction:

While holding a coin in your left hand, show it to the subject and tell her to focus her attention on it. Place it in the center of your right palm, with the head side up. If you leave the coin in your hand long enough while telling her to focus on it, she should see that the head is face up. Closing your hand into a fist, ask her if she thinks the head or tail side of the coin will be facing upward when you open your hand. After answering correctly, open your hand and remove the coin. Have her focus on the coin again but this time instead of placing the coin in your hand drop it into your right hand with the head side up. Again, give her enough time to view which side of the coin is facing up before closing your hand into a fist. Ask her which side of the coin she believes will be displayed when you open your hand. After answering correctly open your hand and remove the coin with your left hand and have her focus her attention on it once more.

This time, instead of dropping the coin onto your palm, grab the coin from your left hand using the French Drop technique. With your left index and middle fingers together, hold the cylindrical edge of the coin with those two fingers and your thumb so it is clearly visible to the subject. Appear to take the coin with the same hand it was previously placed and dropped into, (the right hand), and collapse your fingers so that she thinks the coin is in your right hand. While pretending to hold the coin in your closed fist take a moment to tell her what the definition of an illusion is while also explaining what she just witnessed.

"The dictionary describes the definition of an illusion as an instance of deception, the action of deceiving or misleading. What you just saw was an illusion because when you were asked what side of the coin was facing upward, you were actually wrong because you really didn't see anything at all, because there never was a coin. It was all an illusion just like when you dream and sleep."

The following should take place while you are completing the above words (…dream and sleep.) Lift your closed right hand about eye level. From there open your fingers and display your empty palm while simultaneously saying the word dream. When she looks at your hand and notices that there isn't a coin in it she will be surprised. At this moment you should quickly follow up with the words, "…and sleep!" As you quickly, safely, and gently place your empty hand on her face, you should be covering her eyes and saying the word "sleep."

THE MESMERIZING INDUCTION

Induction:

While standing close to the subject stare deeply into her eyes. In one continuous slow, fluid motion, bring your slightly closed hand up in front of your face and begin moving it toward her face while extending, separating and pointing your index and middle fingers at her eyes. When you reach her eyes, slowly turn and move your hand back towards your face as you point your fingers at your eyes. When your index and middle fingers reach your eyes turn the fingers in her direction and move your hand close to her face while pointing at her eyes. When you get close to her face quickly snap your fingers and loudly command her to sleep.

Note:

Maintain continuous eye contact throughout the induction.

WORD FROM THE AUTHOR

I hope you found pleasure delving into these inductions, finding them useful, fun, and easy to do. My next hypnosis project will be just as equally exciting to work on and I look forward to sharing it with you soon. In the meantime I leave you with a few extra inductions to enjoy.

EXTRA INDUCTIONS

HYPNOTIC GAZE INDUCTION

Induction:

Sitting directly across from the subject, have her put her feet and knees together. Place your knees outside of her legs and knees so the inside of your right foot is beside the outside of her left foot and the inside of your left foot is beside the outside of her right foot. With your elbows close to your ribs, bring your hands in front of your body near your sternum. Your palms should be facing upward and the fingertips should be slightly touching each other. Bring your hands forward towards the subject so they are hovering approximately halfway between the two of you.

Tell the subject to place her hands in your palms. As you lightly hold her hands in your palms have her stare into your eyes. While you gaze into her eyes with minimal to no blinking, remain perfectly still only inhaling and exhaling deeply, slowly, and softly. When she begins to mimic your breathing, at some point when she is near the end of an exhale quickly and carefully tug her arms towards you, commanding her to sleep.

Note:

After commanding her to sleep, slowly and gently sway her arms from side to side as you continue with the deepener.

PALM PUSH INDUCTION

Induction:

Standing face to face in close proximity of the subject, have her place her feet together as you firmly stand with one leg forward and the other one back. Have her bend her right arm and raise her hand in the position as though she is being sworn in. Now have her extend her arm out towards you. Her palm should be facing you and her arm should be slightly bent so she does not hyperextend it. Gaze into the subject's eyes and instruct her to apply a good amount of pressure against your left hand the moment you touch her palm.

Place your right hand on her left shoulder. (Placing your right hand on the subject's shoulder will help you to protect her from falling forward.) Now press your left palm against her right palm. As she begins to increase pressure against your palm, immediately slide your left hand away so her hand, arm, and body shifts slightly towards you, causing her to lose her balance. At this time you should be commanding her to sleep.

FINGERS AND TOES INDUCTION

Induction:

Have the subject sit with her knees and feet together. Tell her to keep her feet flat on the floor, and have her place her hands on her lap. Have her close her eyelids and begin lifting and resting the little toe on her left foot and then the little toe on her right foot and then the little finger on her left hand and then the little finger on her right hand. Have her continue going through the same process with each toe and finger. Every time she completes an entire cycle of lifting and resting all the digits she is to start over.

As the subject proceeds with the task of lifting and lowering the digits, distract her by suggesting relaxation, confusion, and eventually catalepsy of the toes, fingers and eyelids. When you notice the suggestions taking place, persuade her to go into hypnosis.

THE SUBTLE FRACTIONATION TECHNIQUE

Re-induction Deepener:

After hypnotizing the subject with any of the above inductions, tell her that after fifteen seconds of your silence she will begin to take herself out of hypnosis. Continue by telling her that as soon as she hears your voice she will immediately drift right back into hypnosis even deeper than before. When you stop talking wait for her to emerge from hypnosis and as she begins to open her eyelids say, "That's right and go even deeper into hypnosis now." Continue having her emerge from hypnosis by remaining silent, and continue having her enter hypnosis when she hears your voice. Repeat this three to four times.

Before completely emerging the subject out of hypnosis, tell her you will count from one to three and when you reach the number three she will no longer be hypnotized and she will come out of hypnosis feeling good, relaxed and wonderful in every way.

Note:

After counting from one to three the subject should no longer go into hypnosis when hearing your voice as previously suggested. If she happens to go into hypnosis after hearing your voice, have her enter hypnosis and simply cancel the suggestion by telling her she will no longer drift into hypnosis when hearing your voice and everything is back to normal.

Printed in the United States
By Bookmasters